DRAW LIKE AN ANCIENT EGYPTIAN

BY JOE GAMBLE

THE CIVILISATION OF THE ANCIENT
EGYPTIANS LASTED OVER 3000 YEARS.

CLEOPATRA, WHO RULED TOWARDS THE END
OF THAT PERIOD, WAS AS FAR REMOVED
FROM THE CONSTRUCTION OF THE GREAT
PYRAMID AS YOU ARE FROM THE
CONSTRUCTION OF THE PARTHENON.

IN THE BEGINNING THERE WAS NOTHING BUT A LIFELESS SEA. THE SUN GOD RA EMERGED FROM A MOUND AND MADE LAND.

RA AND HIS WIFE, NUT, HAD LOTS OF CHILDREN. HIS FAVOURITE WAS OSIRIS, WHO HE MADE GOD OF THE LAND.

OSIRIS MARRIED ISIS AND THE TWO HAD A SON CALLED HORUS.

OSIRIS'S BROTHER, SETH WAS JEALOUS OF HIM AND KILLED OSIRIS, CHOPPING HIS BODY UP AND THROWING IT FAR ACROSS THE LAND.

WHEN HORUS LEARNED WHAT SETH HAD DONE HE FOUND HIM AND KILLED HIM.

ISIS TRACKED DOWN ALL THE PIECES OF OSIRIS AND PIECED HIM BACK TOGETHER, BUT COULD NOT BRING HIM BACK TO LIFE

RA MADE OSIRIS GOD OF THE UNDERWORLD AND HORUS GOD OF THE LAND

ISIS RETURNS TO THE RIVER EVERY YEAR IN THE AUTUMN TO MOURN THE DEATH OF HER HUSBAND. AS HER TEARS FALL, THE NILE SWELLS.

EGYPTIAN GODS

SHU

God of wind and air. He is a calming, peaceful god

RA

The all powerful sun god Ra has the head of a hawk. He called all living beings into life by speaking their secret names.

TEFNUT

Sister and wife of Shu, Tefnut is goddess of rain and moisture. She has the face of a lion. She is the mother of Geb and Nut.

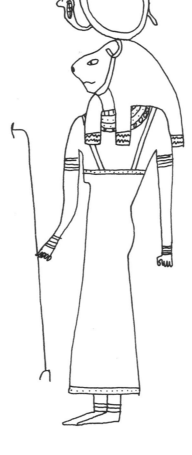

NUT

Goddess of the sky, wife of Geb and mother to Osiris, Isis and Set. She carries a pot on her head and sometimes takes the form of a cow.

GEB

God of the earth and father of snakes, Geb makes crops grow.

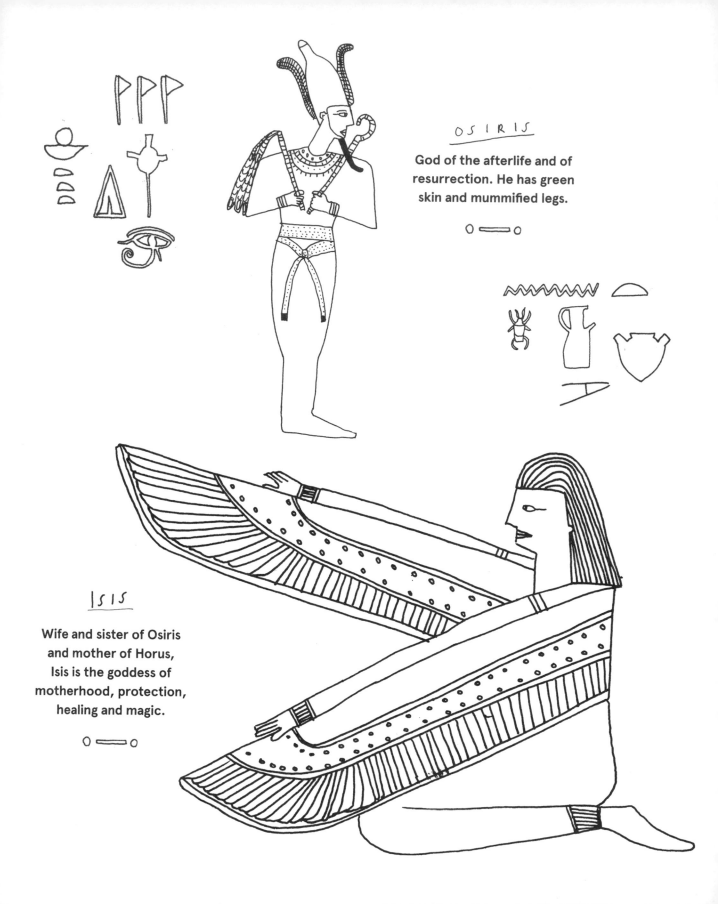

OSIRIS

God of the afterlife and of resurrection. He has green skin and mummified legs.

ISIS

Wife and sister of Osiris and mother of Horus, Isis is the goddess of motherhood, protection, healing and magic.

ANUBIS

Anubis is protector of graves and god of embalming. He has the head of a jackal, as jackals were always seen around graves.

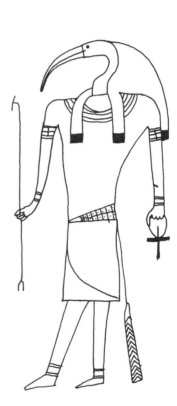

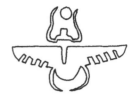

HORUS

Falcon-headed Horus is god of the sky, war and kingship, and protector of Egypt. Day turns to night when Horus the falcon flies across the sky.

THOTH

With the head of an ibis, Thoth is the god of science and time. He maintains the balance between good and evil, creating harmony in the universe.

DRAW YOURSELF AND YOUR FAMILY
AS EGYPTIAN GODS.

WHAT ANIMALS REPRESENT YOU?

WHAT WOULD YOUR POWERS BE?

BA & KA

THE ANCIENT EGYPTIANS BELIEVED THAT YOUR SOUL SPLIT INTO TWO PARTS AFTER YOU DIED. THE BA IS YOUR PERSONALITY — EVERYTHING THAT MAKES YOU _YOU_. THE KA IS YOUR LIFE FORCE.

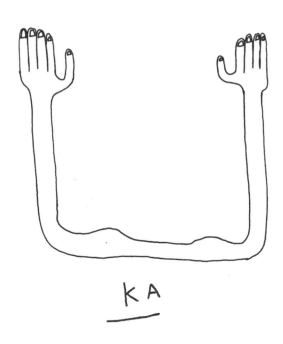

KA

After death, the BA flies off every morning to keep watch over your loved ones, whilst the KA flies to the land of the dead. At night, the two parts of your soul are reunited in your mummified body.

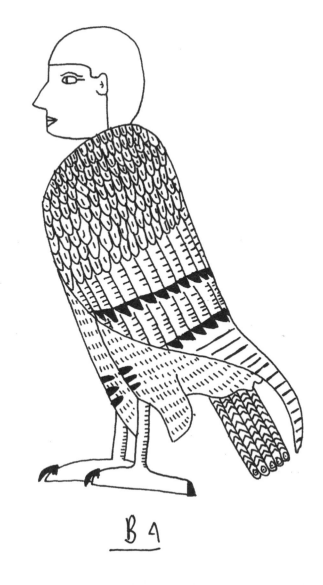

BA

If the Ba and Ka cannot return to the body, they suffer a second and final death. This is why it was of the utmost importance that the body was preserved.

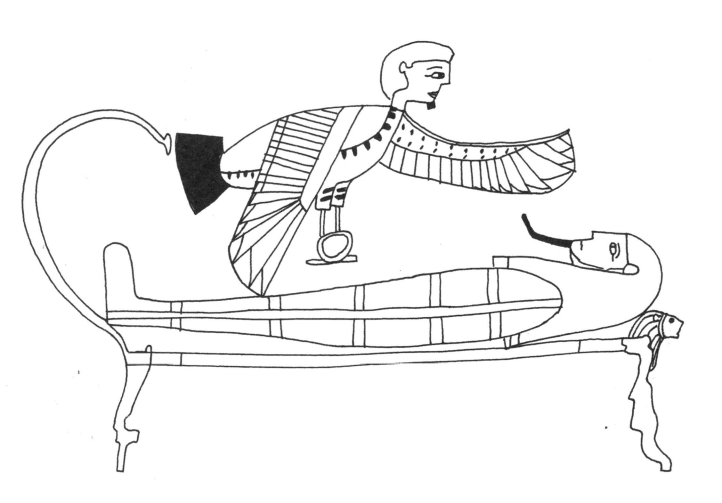

CANOPIC JARS

HOW TO MAKE A MUMMY STEP 1:
REMOVE ALL THE ORGANS
EXCEPT THE HEART AND PUT
THEM INTO MAGICAL JARS
IN THE SHAPE OF THE FOUR
SONS OF HORUS.

JACKAL-HEADED DUAMUTE
GUARDS THE STOMACH

BABOON-HEADED HAPY
GUARDS THE LUNGS

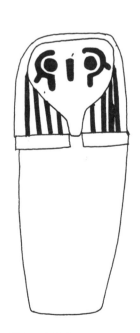

FALCON-HEADED QEBEHSENUEF
GUARDS THE INTESTINES

HUMAN-HEADED IMSETY
GUARDS THE LIVER

DESIGN YOUR OWN CANOPIC JARS HERE

MUMMIES!

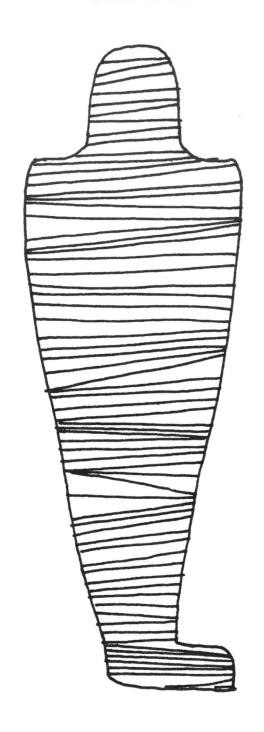

HOW TO MAKE A MUMMY   STEP 2:
DRY THE BODY OUT USING SPECIAL SALT
AND WRAP IT IN LONG STRIPS OF LINEN.

PLACE A DEATH MASK ON TOP IN THE LIKENESS OF THE PERSON WHO DIED, SO THAT THE BA RETURNS TO THE RIGHT BODY.

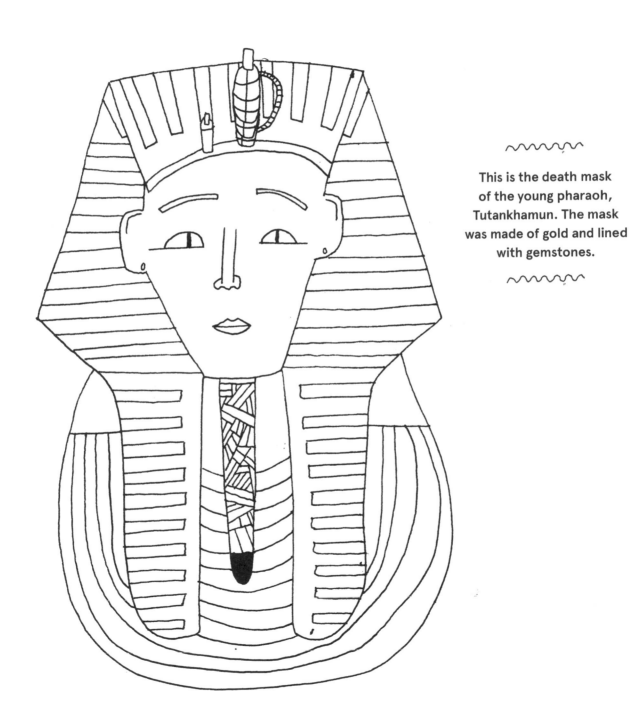

This is the death mask of the young pharaoh, Tutankhamun. The mask was made of gold and lined with gemstones.

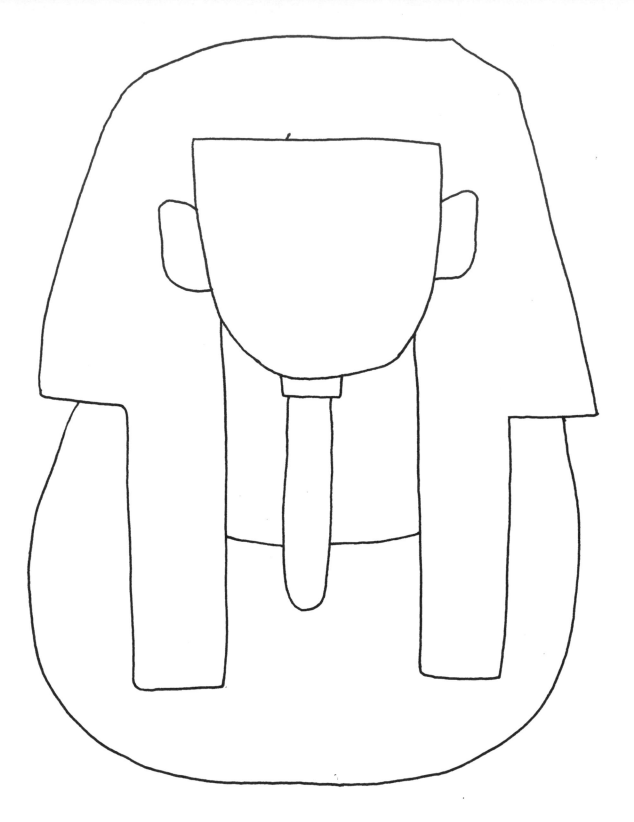

DRAW THE FACES ON THESE DEATH
MASKS AND DECORATE THEM WITH PATTERNS AND JEWELS!

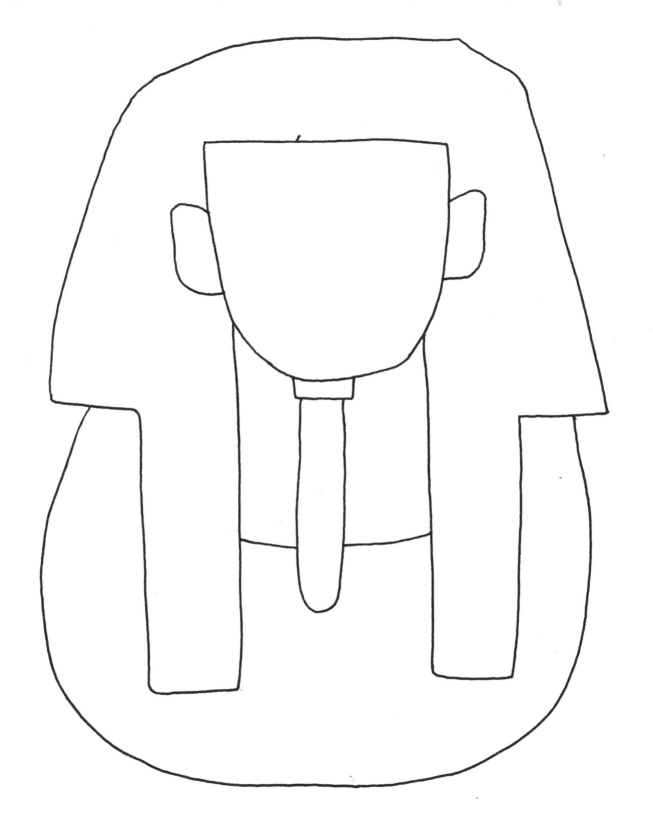

HOW TO MAKE A MUMMY STEP 3:

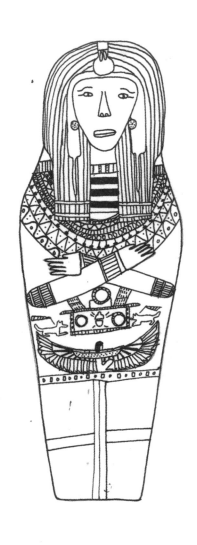
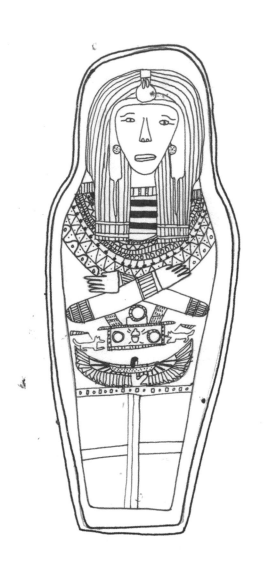

PUT THE MUMMY IN A DECORATED WOODEN COFFIN
PUT THE COFFIN IN ANOTHER COFFIN WITH
MORE HIEROGLYPHICS AND DECORATION

PUT THE COFFINS INSIDE A STONE SARCOPHAGUS
CARVED WITH MAGICAL SPELLS, PAINTINGS
OF BATTLES AND SACRED ANIMALS AND EYES, SO
THAT THE BODY COULD SEE OUT

DECORATE THESE COFFINS.

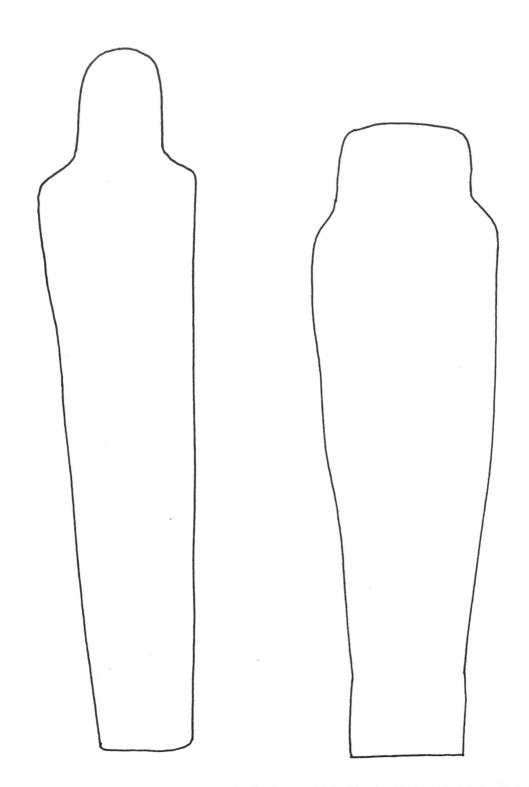

DECORATE THE SARCOPHAGUS!
WHAT STORIES WOULD YOU DEPICT FROM YOUR LIFE?
WHAT ANIMALS WOULD BE SACRED TO YOU?

HIEROGLYPHICS

THE EGYPTIANS USED OVER 2000 HIEROGLYPHIC CHARACTERS!

THIS IS A SIMPLIFIED HIEROGLYPHIC ALPHABET.

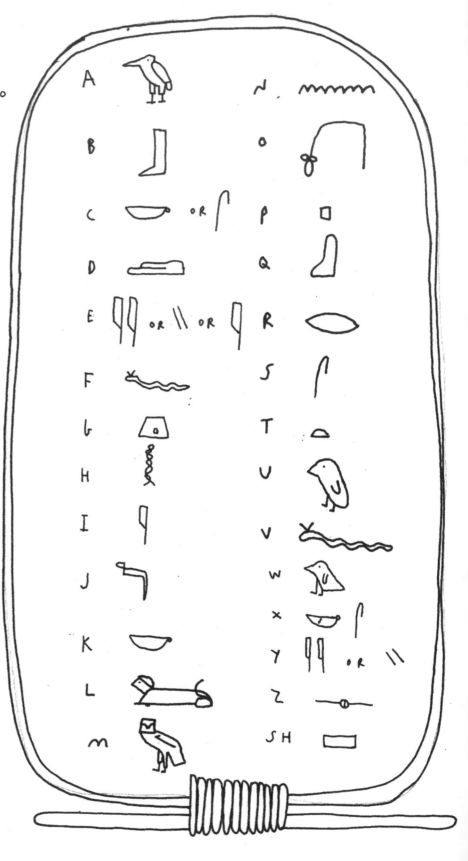

Ancient Egyptians believed that each person had a true name, called a REN. If people stopped using your ren, you would die a second death and never reach the afterlife.

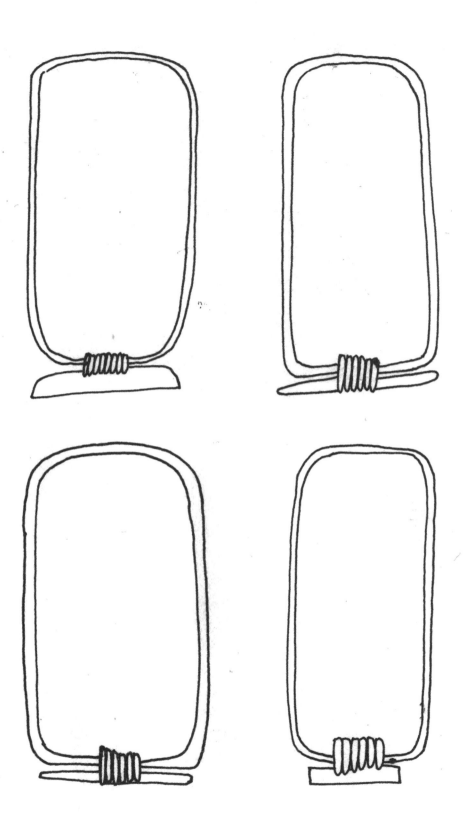

Therefore it was
important to write your
ren inside a magical rope
to protect it. This rope
was called a cartouche.

WRITE YOUR NAME INSIDE A CARTOUCHE.

DRAW LIKE AN EGYPTIAN

THE BODY IS DRAWN FROM A FRONTAL VIEW —

TWO SHOULDERS

TWO ARMS

THE FACE IS IN PROFILE — ONE EYE, ONE NOSE

THE LEGS AND FEET ARE IN PROFILE. OFTEN WITH TWO LEFT FEET.

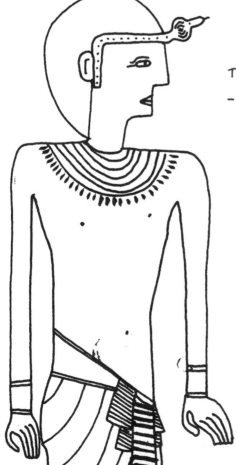

DRAW LIKE AN EGYPTIAN HERE!

Proportion was very important. Use these guidelines to get it right.

Only six colours were used, blue, green, white, black, red and yellow.

SYMBOLS

WAS SCEPTER
An animal-headed scepter that symbolises godly power

NTJR
An axe representing godliness

ANKH
Represents eternal life

0000

The gods and pharaohs were often depicted carrying or surrounded by symbolic objects:

0000

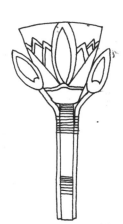

LOTUS FLOWER
Symbolises rebirth

CROOK
Stands for kingship

DJED
A column representing stability

EYE OF HORUS
The most powerful symbol of protection and healing

FLAIL
Represents Osiris and fertility of the land

OUROBORUS
The snake eating its own tail represents eternity

DESIGN SOME MYSTICAL SYMBOLS THAT CAPTURE
YOUR VERY ESSENCE.

BOOK OF THE DEAD

THE BOOK OF THE DEAD WAS A SERIES OF SCROLLS THAT WERE BURIED N THE TOMBS FILLED WITH PASSWORDS, SPELLS AND PRAYERS THAT WOULD HELP THE SOUL THROUGH THE MAZES AND OBSTACLES ON THE WAY TO THE AFTERLIFE.

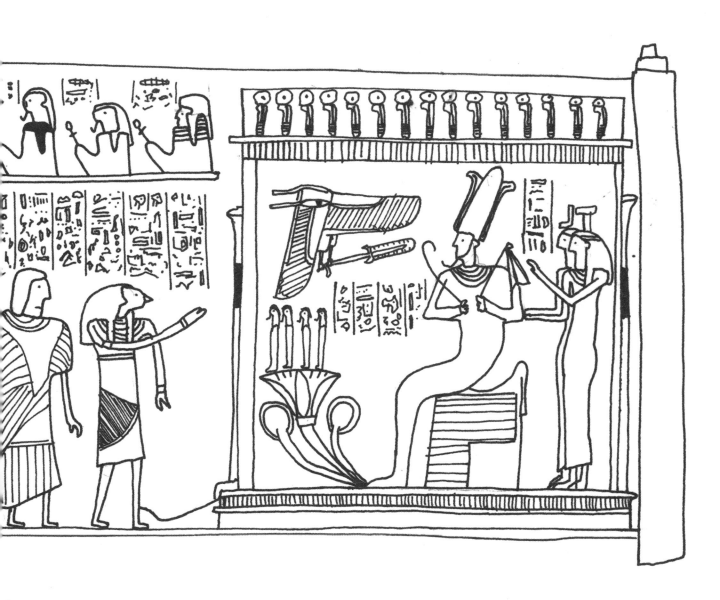

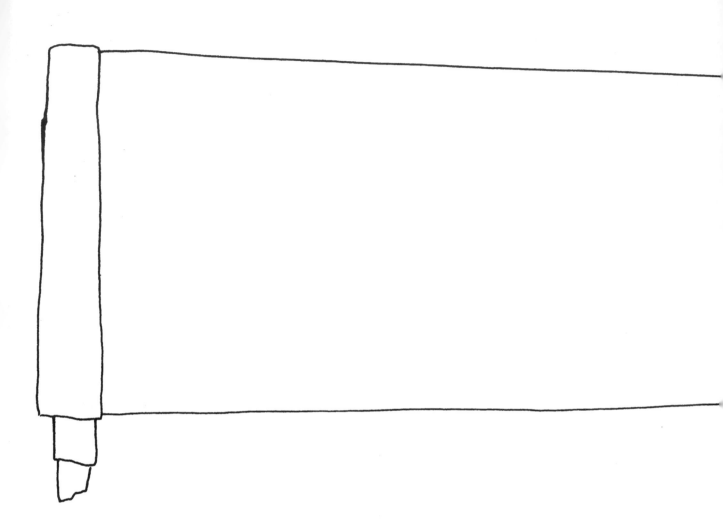

DRAW PROTECTIVE SPELLS FOR YOURSELF AND YOUR FAMILY. USE HIEROGLYPHICS, SYMBOLS AND EGYPTIAN DRAWING SKILLS.

AMULETS

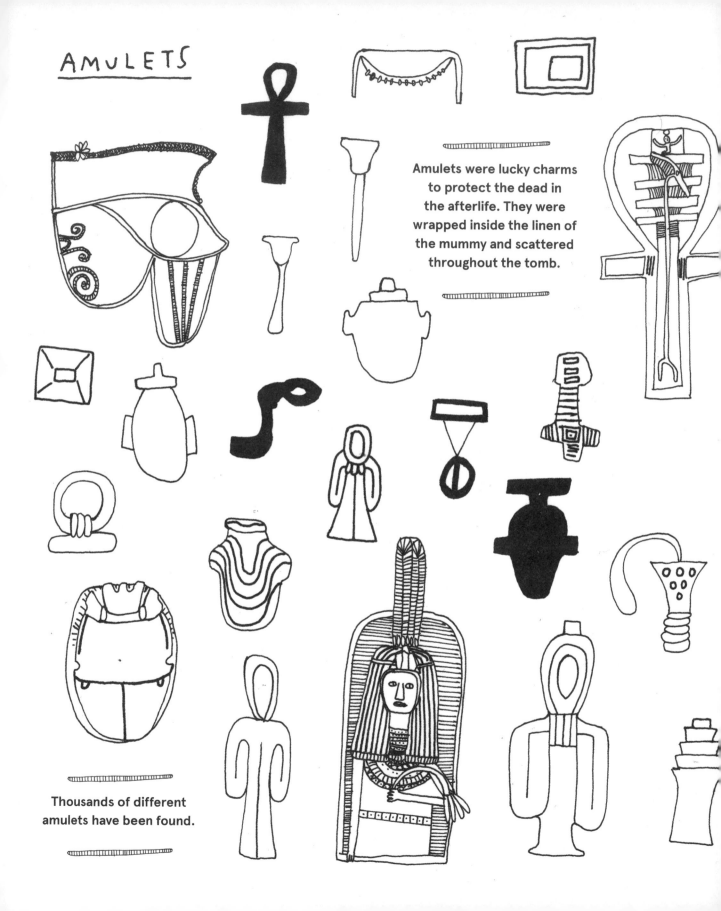

Amulets were lucky charms to protect the dead in the afterlife. They were wrapped inside the linen of the mummy and scattered throughout the tomb.

Thousands of different amulets have been found.

DESIGN SOME AMULETS FOR PROTECTION.

SCARABS

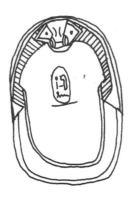

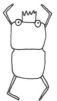

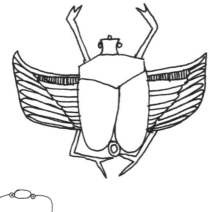

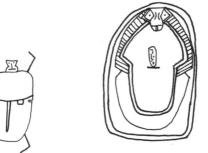

Scarab amulets were
particularly popular. The
scarab is a dung beetle
that lays its eggs inside
animal dung. When the eggs
hatch the young beetles
eat the dung and emerge
from it fully formed. This
symbolised rebirth.

CAN YOU DRAW A SCARAB?

THE MYSTERY OF THE PYRAMIDS

~~~~~~

Inside there were lots of chambers and passages. We don't know what these were all for, but probably so that the soul could easily enter and exit the tomb.

~~~~~~

~~~~~~

The pyramids were huge tombs built in the desert.

~~~~~~

The Great Pyramid of Giza was the biggest of all. It is thought that it was once faced with white stone with a gold tip that caught the sun and shone out across the desert.

~~~~~~

AIR SHAFT

AIR SHAFT

GRAND GALLERY

KINGS CHAMBER

QUEENS CHAMBER

AIR SHAFT

AIR SHAFT

SUBTERRANEAN CHAMBER

BLUEPRINT OF THE GREAT PYRAMID OF GIZA

DESIGN YOUR OWN PYRAMID.
WHAT CHAMBERS ARE IN THERE?
WHAT PURPOSES DO THEY SERVE?

GRAVE GOODS

THE EGYPTIANS BELIEVED THAT THE THINGS
THAT WERE REQUIRED IN LIFE WERE
ALSO REQUIRED IN DEATH

BOARD GAMES

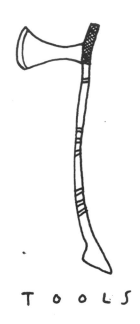

TOOLS

COMBS

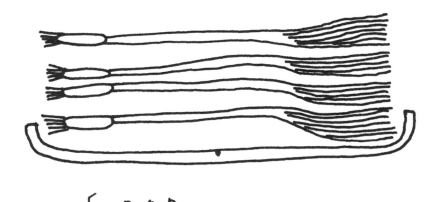

FOOD

CLOTHES

FURNITURE

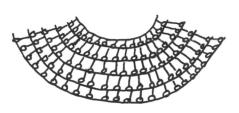

JEWELLERY

BASKETS

SHABTI DOLLS

(THESE WERE TINY SCULPTURES OF SERVANTS WHO WOULD WORK FOR THEIR MASTER IN THE AFTERLIFE)

TAKING IT WITH YOU

WHAT OBJECTS AND PEOPLE DO YOU VALUE IN LIFE?

WHAT WOULD YOU WANT TO TAKE TO THE AFTERLIFE?

CATS

CATS BIG AND SMALL WERE CONSIDERED SACRED. THEY WERE THOUGHT TO HAVE MAGICAL POWERS TO PROTECT CHILDREN AND HOMES.

When a cat died, the owner would shave off their eyebrows as a sign of mourning. Anyone who killed a cat was sentenced to death.

PET LIONS WERE KEPT
BY THE PHARAOH AS
A SIMBOL OF RA.

BASTET WAS THE
GODDESS OF CATS.

THE SPHINX GUARDED
THE GREAT PYRAMIDS
OF GIZA.

DRAW SOME COOL CATS WEARING PLENTY
OF JEWELLERY

HEAD DRESSES

Whilst normal people did not wear headdresses, pharaohs and gods were depicted with some pretty fancy headgear

URAEUS

A rearing cobra that featured on many headdresses

⊐⊐▢

HEDJET CROWN

The white crown of Upper Egypt

⊐⊐▢

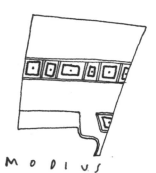

MODIUS

A flat-topped cylindrical headdress of queens and goddesses

⊐⊐▢

DESHRET CROWN

The red crown of Lower Egypt

⊐⊐▢

ATEF CROWN

A Hedjet crown with ostrich feathers on either side, worn by Osiris

⊐⊐▢

NEMES

The striped headdress of the pharaohs

⊐⊐▢

PSCHENT CROWN

Combines the Deshret and the Hedjet crowns to symbolise a unified Egypt

⊐⊐▢

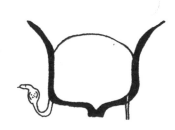

ISIS CROWN

Isis wears a crown of a sun disk with cow horns on either side

⊐⊐▢

DESIGN A HEADDRESS FOR YOURSELF HERE

BEARDS

PHARAOHS WERE CLEAN SHAVEN, BUT THEY WORE FALSE BEARDS.
EVEN FEMALE PHARAOHS WORE THEM!
IN LIFE THEY WORE A PLAITED STRAIGHT BEARD
THAT WAS TIED ONTO THEIR HEADS.

IN DEATH THE BEARD WAS NARROWER, AND CURLED UPWARDS.

DRAW YOURSELF WITH A FALSE BEARD.

DRAW LIKE AN EGYPTIAN
Published by Cicada Books Limited

Illustrated by Joseph Gamble
Design by April

British Library Cataloguing-in-Publication Data.

A CIP record for this book is available from
the British Library.
ISBN: 978-1-908714-49-7

Ꮯ꘠

Cicada Books Limited
48 Burghley Road
London NW5 1UE
E: cicadabooks@gmail.com
W: www.cicadabooks.co.uk